IMAGES
of America

NEW
PROVIDENCE

The New Providence, NJ, Borough Seal.

IMAGES
of America

NEW PROVIDENCE

Joan Gonczlik and Jane Coddington

ARCADIA

Published by Arcadia Publishing,
an imprint of Tempus Publishing, Inc.
2 Cumberland Street
Charleston, SC 29401

Printed in Great Britain.

Library of Congress Catalog Card Number: 98-86140

For all general information contact Arcadia Publishing at:
Telephone 843-853-2070
Fax 843-853-0044
E-Mail arcadia@charleston.net

For customer service and orders:
Toll-Free 1-888-313-BOOK

Visit us on the internet at http://www.arcadiaimages.com

Prepared by Joan Gonczlik and Jane Coddington
(with Dwight Boud, consultant/proofreader)
from materials of the New Providence Historical Society
in celebration of
the Borough of New Providence Centennial Celebration, 1999.

Cover picture found on page 118.

CONTENTS

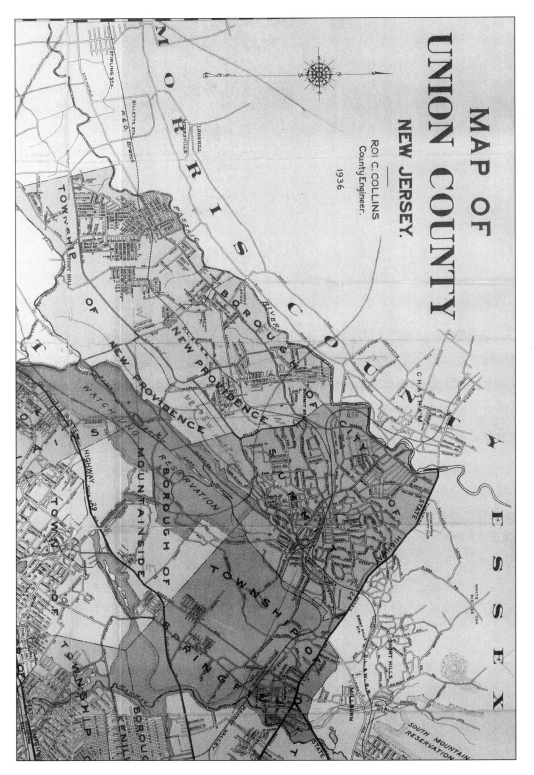

INTRODUCTION

New Providence has evolved over three hundred years from a sparse Puritan settlement to a dynamic town. Its government has changed with its growth, as have all facets of everyday life. Formerly Springfield Township, the area became New Providence Township in 1809 and included present-day Summit (which seceded from New Providence Township in 1869 because of disputes of town management and rapid growth due to its excellent railroad facilities) and Berkeley Heights (which was New Providence Township from 1899 to 1952).

Some excellent histories are available on the area, including: Scott Schultz, *New Jersey Beginnings*; Frank Orleans, *A History*; and *New Providence Fire Department 75th Anniversary Book*.

The New Providence Historical Society hopes this pictorial history will bring joy to its readers as they re-live history, learn of their ancestors, and gain an appreciation of what life was like in those earlier years. The time line which follows gives some historical highlights.

The Historical Society of New Providence has published this book for the centennial year celebration. Our thanks go to the many families whose foresight saved family photos and to those who generously donated them to our archives.

Time Line

Chronological History of New Providence

1664 Land purchased from Native Americans by James, Duke of York, brother to King Charles II
1720 First settlers in the area
1737 Presbyterian Church formed
1759 First use of the name "New Providence"
1793 Becomes Springfield Township
1798 Methodist Episcopal Church formed
1809 Becomes New Providence Township
      (included present-day Summit and Berkeley Heights)
1840 First election
1845 Feltville section built
1857 Union County formed from Essex County
1869 Summit seceded and the Academy built (the first school building)
1891 St. Luke's Reformed Episcopal Church built
1899 New Providence Borough formed
1902 Fire Department formed
1905 Feltville becomes Glenside Park
1907 Lincoln School built, the Academy building becomes Borough Hall
1918 Our Lady of Peace Church began a mission
1912 Free Public Library formed
1943 William Paca Club formed
1951 New Providence Township becomes Berkeley Heights
1954 New Our Lady of Peace Church and school built,
      Hillview (first neighborhood school) built
1957 Faith Lutheran Church built
1958 High School built
1960 St. Andrews Episcopal Church built
1964 Tercentenary (three hundred years)
1999 Centennial of New Providence Borough

One
BOROUGH VIEWS

This is a view of the center of New Providence, looking east on Springfield Avenue, probably around the 1820s. James Badgley is in the buggy. The highest sign reads "Union Hotel, W.J. Post." The farthest sign reads "John F. Wahl, Blacksmith." The house on the right was a Wilcox house and burned sometime before 1902. The first house is now a shoe repair shop, and the second one is partly living quarters with a small shop on the west side. The large pole on the left is the Revolutionary Pole installed during the Revolution.

This is Springfield Avenue looking west toward the center of town, as seen from the front of Lincoln School. The Totten-Balcom House is on the right. (Cornelius Lovell, photographer; courtesy of George Lewis.)

Looking at the northeast corner of the center of town, the first house was, at one time or another, a tavern, stagecoach stop, and ice cream parlor, and was later remodeled into Center Stationers. The first senior citizens met in the room on the right side. The pole on the left is the Revolutionary Pole, on top of which is now the flagpole on the front lawn of Salt Box Museum. (Courtesy of Gus Furneld.)

The former Union Hotel, tavern, and ice cream parlor is pictured here. The sign on the building reads, "Geo. L. Burnett, Cigars & Cigarettes." The standing sign reads, "Sandwiches, Ice Cream, Soda, Candy." (Courtesy of Anne Osborne.)

Looking east on Springfield Avenue to the center of New Providence, the house on the right was the original Academy, built on church property on Passaic Street. It later served as the church parish house until about 1913, when it was moved to this location. It has since served as the library, the Junior Order of Mechanics Hall, Balcom Parcells Hardware Store, and Leisure Travel. The next building (to the left of the original Academy building) was the first firehouse and has had various occupants. The Village Store on the corner has been replaced by a parking lot. Pictured below is the same building complex in the 1950s. (Courtesy of George Lewis.)

12

This is the center of New Providence, looking from Passaic Street up South Street. Note the horse and buggy beside the store. The Wilcox house is in the center of the picture. (Courtesy of John Hickson.)

Here is the mill on South Street, where the Exxon Service Station is now located. Elsie Parcells Jacobus and Leon Parcells are in the picture. (Courtesy of George Lewis.)

Pictured here is the Crane Store, *c.* 1896, located on the south side of Springfield Avenue, where the Madonna Building was once located. Pictured from left to right are: Will Crane, Jim Horner, Mr. Barber (with beard), Frank Wahl (boy), and Oscar Dickinson. The sign over the door reads "Township Committee Room." Mr. Peck took over the store about 1907, but Mr. Crane probably still owned it. About 1919 the store was sold to Mr. Weid for his butcher shop. (Courtesy of George Lewis.)

The first farmer's market, owned by David Totten, is shown here. David Totten's granddaughter, Mae Woodruff, is in this photograph. (Courtesy of George Lewis.)

The Charles M. Decker & Brothers store was located on the north side of Springfield Avenue next to the gas station. This was a chain store run by William Totten. The people shown are Henry Petroski (left) and William Totten. One side was used for a classroom in 1915, with Miss Ethel Hickson as teacher and Allen W. Roberts as a member of the class. The Borough Library was in the store on the left. (George Valentine Howard, photographer; courtesy of John Hickson.)

Frank B. Totten owned and lived in this building, which he purchased for $600 and eventually sold for $30,000. He operated a poolroom and sold soft drinks and candy. (George Valentine Howard, photographer; courtesy of C. Ernie Fischer.)

The Village Store, owned by Wilcox, Parcells, Behre, and Blatt, was located on what is now the parking lot of Summit Bank. It was also the post office and general meeting place around a pot-bellied stove. (George Valentine Howard, photographer.)

The Attridg house was remodeled by Mr. Macaluso about 1920 and was the first delicatessen in New Providence. (George Valentine Howard, photographer; courtesy of Anne Osborne.)

The Evergreen Hotel was the first hotel in New Providence and was located at 15 Southgate Road in 1898. (Courtesy of George Lewis.)

Bert Abbazia is seen posing by his new Done Well Cleaner truck. (Courtesy of Abbazia.)

Ernie Fischer is in the Renault with Augie Engel standing in front of the Fischer garage, c. 1940. A diner is presently located on the site. (Courtesy of George Lewis.)

This post office at "West Summit" (then New Providence) was located on Springfield Avenue across from Pittsford Way around 1900. (Courtesy of George Lewis.)

The oldest Murray Hill Post Office was located near the Murray Hill Train Station up until the 1950s. Pictured from left to right are: Ruth and Esther Alpaugh, Dorothy Badgley, and Margaret Adams. (Courtesy of C. Ernie Fischer.)

Dorothy McGrath, Postmistress Rose Ricci, and Sal Allocco are all crowded into the old, "smallest" post office in 1954. (Courtesy of Marie Ricci.)

Mr. Burnett is shown standing beside his cider mill, which he purchased in 1876. The building began as a tannery in 1818, became a feed mill until 1858, and then was used in manufacturing novelty wood and block articles. Since cider is seasonal, Mr. Burnett rented space out to a rug maker. The cider was known far and wide as "the best." (Courtesy of George Lewis.)

Before supermarkets, this delivery wagon, with Tony Gallo driving, made the rounds with groceries, vegetables, and ice cream. (Courtesy of George Lewis.)

Tony Gallo and family are seen in front of his house and store, which was incorporated into historic Murray Hill Square. (Courtesy of George Lewis.)

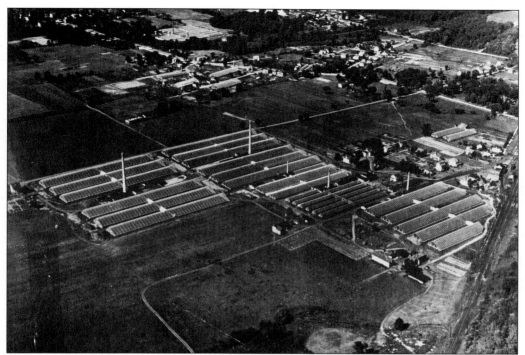

This is an aerial view of the Coddington Greenhouses, which were built along the railroad tracks shown to the right. L.B. Coddington began his business here in the late 1800s and had more acres under glass than any other grower. He specialized in roses and gardenias. (Courtesy of George Lewis.)

One of several celebrity days featuring Coddington roses is pictured here. L.B. Coddington Jr. is on the left, with movie star Betty Hutton in the center. (Courtesy of Coddington.)

Shown here are some of the Coddington workers' two-family houses, which were removed to make room for historic Murray Hill Square. (Mabel Henshaw, photographer; courtesy of George Lewis.)

Members of the Coddington work force pose for an unusual picture in 1924. Among some of the workers pictured here, from left to right, are as follows: (first row) Charles Mastrobono (third from left) and George Filo (fifth from left); (second row) Pasquale Proccacini, Carmine "Joe" Mazzucco, Harry Pictroski, and Mr. Pastore (to the right of the post); (third row) Mr. Gennetti (third from left) and Salvatore Allocco (fourth from left); (fourth row) Peter Parlapiano (on the far right); (back row) Dominick Rosato (second from left), Sam Parlapiano (fifth from left), and Thomas Friola (seventh from left). (Courtesy of Ida Peca.)

24

This gas station is Harry's Mobil, located on Springfield Avenue across from what is now Union Avenue. It is interesting to see how undeveloped the area was only a few years ago. (Courtesy of Ida Bartholomew.)

In the early 1900s, there was an active stone quarry on Maple Street. Pictured here, from left to right, are: Fred Stahl, unidentified, Kitty Stahl, unidentified, and Ted Stahl. During the 1940s, some local residents used the extinct quarry for target practice. Homes now surround the area. (Courtesy of George Lewis.)

These pictures show our town before development. The top photograph is Central Avenue, west of Maple Street, looking east. Pictured below is a view looking down Mountain Avenue toward Summit. To the left is Maple Street. (Courtesy of Anne Osborne.)

A work crew is shown installing sewers at South Street and Oakwood Drive in 1948. Frank B. Mason (third from left) was the inspector responsible for laying the sewers and the first operator of the sewer disposal plant. (Courtesy of Mary Mason.)

This picture was taken from the porch of a Glenside Road home and shows a view of Bell Labs property, which was bought by Bell Labs in 1930. The labs were begun in 1940. C.T. Boyle, a member of the Bell Labs staff, lived in the house until the property was developed. The grove of trees in the distant center is the property on which the Allstate Insurance Company built their headquarters. (Courtesy of Bell Labs.)

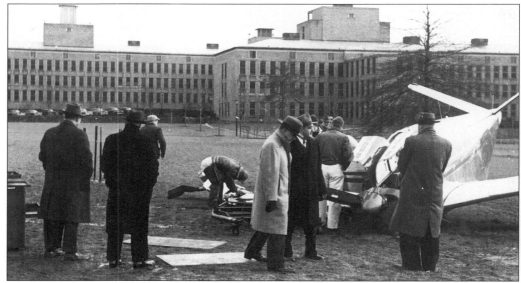

In 1954, this small plane crashed in New Providence on the front lawn of Bell Labs. The picture shows how the property looked before it was fully developed. (Courtesy of Allen W. Roberts.)

Two
SECURITY AND TRANSPORTATION

The first New Providence fire apparatus was a horse-drawn hook-and-ladder, with hose reels pulled by men. It was used prior to 1913. This firehouse was on Springfield Avenue. (Courtesy of George Lewis.)

In 1914, a mechanized fire engine was purchased by the town for $700. The body was from the Morristown Fire Department. The Borough Council provided $400, and the firemen raised $300. (Courtesy of John Hickson.)

An early fire department photograph. Pictured here, from left to right, are as follows: (front row) Wallace Parcells, E.W. Baldwin, Walter Behre, O.F. Adams, S. Horvath, A. Bradley, and F. Weid Sr.; (back row) C. Terry, T. Sorman, L. Adams, F. Weid Jr., J. Smith, C. Ernie Fischer, and F. Meyers. (Courtesy of C. Ernie Fischer.)

John Parker is sitting on the old fire ring at the Presbyterian church, with the cemetery visible in the background. (Courtesy of Sophie Miller.)

The Sanford fire truck was purchased in 1929. It was sold in 1946 to the fire department in Summit, New York, for $1,300. (Courtesy of Hugh Jordan.)

A large group of fire department friends and family gathered for the annual picnic in 1932. (Courtesy of George Lewis.)

No. 81

Union County
LICENSE
TO

Exempt members of any volunteer fire department, volunteer fire ~~engine, hook~~ and ladder, hose, supply company, or salvage corps of the cities, towns, boroughs, townships and fire districts in this state, for hawking, peddling and vending of merchandise within this state.

This is to Certify, That _Halsey Genung_

presented to me his Exemption Certificate, from the _Boro of New_ ~~Providence~~

Fire Dept *of the* _County of Union_,

New Jersey, he is hereby licensed to hawk, peddle and vend any goods, wares or merchandise or solicit trade within this State, and is entitled to all the benefits allowed under Chapter 133, Laws, Session of 1911.

Given under my hand and Official Seal,

this 26th *day of* May
*A.D., 19*32

Neil McLeod Jr.
COUNTY CLERK

Members of the fire department had unusual benefits early in the century.

The New Providence Fire Department upgraded during the 1930s by purchasing its first pumper. In the truck, pictured from left to right, are: Larry Osborne, William Smith, and C. Ernie Fischer. (Courtesy of C. Ernie Fischer.)

Bill Vignali proudly shows off one of the newer engines. (Courtesy of Marie Allocco.)

John (Jake) Miller is pictured here. He was a constable of the Union County Court before being named a marshall of New Providence. (Courtesy of Sophie Miller.)

The uniform of Chief of Police James Morgan indicates how "ready for action" he was, although New Providence was still quite small. (Courtesy of George Lewis.)

This "used" Cadillac sedan was purchased in 1937 and renovated by the firemen for use by the first aid squad. (Courtesy of Hugh Jordan.)

Among the school guards shown with Harry High are children from the Osborne, Rosato, Parlapiano, and Paradiso families. (Courtesy of Bertha High.)

Pictured, from left to right, are James Venezia, Harry High, Carl Ehnis, and Richard Schmitt. They are on the lawn of the former Academy, where the police station was then located. (Courtesy of Bertha High.)

Hazel and Anna Attridg, using an 1800s method of seeing the town, enjoy driving in the Fourth-of-July parade. (Courtesy of Anne Osborne.)

This is an 1888 photograph of the first New Providence railroad station. The railroad crossed Springfield Avenue. This portion of town was then called West Summit. (Courtesy of Lovell.)

In the early 1900s, this Murray Hill railroad station was built a short distance west of the original station. (Courtesy of Jane Parcells.)

The Elkwood railroad station in West Summit was moved to Passaic Avenue and became a private residence. (Courtesy of Jane Parcells.)

The Passaic Street bridge remained a narrow structure from the early 1900s into the early 1970s. (Courtesy of John Hickson.)

The May 1958 flood made crossing the Passaic River a hazardous experience. (Courtesy of R.S. Kennedy.)

Michael DeCorso owned this bus in the 1920s. The sign on the bus says, "North New Providence via Berkeley Heights." (Courtesy of Lucy DeCorso.)

Mr. and Mrs. DeCorso pose with his new yellow bus in the 1960s. The routing of the bus shows Union Avenue, New Providence. (Courtesy of R.S. Kennedy.)

Blizzards in the late 1920s posed a challenge to residents. Many volunteered to help clean roadways. Pictured above are horses pulling a primitive plow. Pictured below is a road crew which includes Linden Adams, Raymond Parks, Wallace Parcells, Fred Coddington, and Art Peck. (Courtesy of Sophie Miller.)

Frequent flooding of the Salt Brook held up traffic on Springfield Avenue. This was in the 1930s before the Salt Brook was brought under control. (Courtesy of A.W. Roberts.)

Harry Wellbourne, a local fireman, proudly drives his early-1900s car, back when roads were a challenge. (Courtesy of John Hickson.)

Here was a new sight on the roads: a Public Service Gas Company vehicle. With no windows, would you like his job in the winter? (Courtesy of Sophie Miller.)

This beautiful horse-drawn buggy makes us nostalgic. The picture was taken on Maple Street, near the quarry, around 1904. (Courtesy of George Lewis.)

A slight contrast from the horse and buggy is this Maxwell car owned by L.B. Coddington Sr. (Courtesy of Audrey Coddington.)

Michael DeCorso's bus line grew through the 1950s. Vito Sabia Sr. is shown in 1952 driving for the bus line. (Courtesy of Rosemarie Sabia Cucco.)

Mike DeCorso, Bill MacNamara, and Tony Beatrice are pictured outside DeCorso's garage in 1930. (Courtesy of Tran Beatrice.)

In the 1940s, the Murray Hill station was the scene of a train derailment, beside the old post office and the coal pockets, which are still beside the tracks. All the green house coal was received through them. (Courtesy of Audrey Coddington.)

Three
HOMES

This was the home of Samuel C. Parcells at 44 South Street in 1890. Margaret Parcells is holding Leon G. Parcells, and Oscar Badgley is sitting with her. Faitoute Agency has occupied the building for many years. (Courtesy of Anne Osborne.)

Deborah Marshall Brant was born in 1813 at 410 Union Avenue. She was a devout Methodist and gave the first $50 toward the building of the church. She is buried in the New Providence Methodist Cemetery. Deborah was the mother of Mary Alice Nason. (Courtesy of A.W. Roberts.)

This home is believed to be the oldest house in New Providence and is located at 161 Mountain Avenue. Former owners are Doty, Hill, and Harboe.

An old home, typical of the 1800s, was the Nason family home at 471 Union Avenue. (Courtesy of A.W. Roberts; from the estate of Bertha Roberts Nason.)

A postal card shows the Polly Watkins Childrens' Home. The Childrens' Home moved to Summit, and Miss Boiney and Miss Bretiner continued to own the home. Later, Miss Florence Watson, who lived there as an orphan, became the owner. The house was torn down in 1998.

The David Harrison Totten family is pictured in front of their home on Springfield Avenue in 1890. Pictured here, from left to right, are Wesley (sitting with the dog), Dr. H. Totten Sr. (standing by the tree), Frank (holding Phoebe on his lap), Gussie H., David W., Mrs. Abby Bedford Totten (holding William), Charles S., Jane N., and Ida Vell. (Courtesy of George Lewis.)

Located at 51 Woodland Road and the corner of South Street, this home can be traced back to 1845, when Henry Wilcox lived here. Later, the Hartshorns, the Riccis, and then the Kesslers owned the property. When the property was re-landscaped, many artifacts were found, including farm implements, hair dye, and a bottle saying, "Bumsteads Worm Syrup." (Courtesy of Anne Osborne.)

This home, at 187 Passaic Street, was known as the Barrell house. It was later owned by the Osbornes. This photo was taken in the 1890s. (Courtesy of George Lewis.)

The "House of Seven Gables" is now 1976 Springfield Avenue. In the early 1900s, Simon Wahl lived here and had a blacksmith shop in the back. (Courtesy of George Lewis.)

Before the streets were paved, this was a view of Springfield Avenue showing the Stover house across from Maple Street. This photo was taken in 1888, and the former owners included Runyon, Stover, Evans, Blondin, and Jones. (Courtesy of C. Lovell.)

This lovely old home at 939 Springfield Avenue is still being treasured by its family. (Courtesy of A. Schwalzwalder.)

Mr. and Mrs. John L. Deen owned the fashionable Murray Hill home (shown on the facing page) in the mid-1800s. (Courtesy of Martha Olive.)

The Deen's home was turned into a clubhouse and their surrounding land became the Murray Hill Golf Club. (Courtesy of John Hickson.)

The Frank and Mary Mason home at 1377 Springfield Avenue is currently owned and occupied by their daughter, Dorothy Mason, who was one of the principle donors to the new Historical Society Room in the New Providence Memorial Library. (Courtesy of George Lewis.)

At 64 South Street was the home of John and Nettie Hedges Badgley in the early 1900s. John Badgley was the son of Dayton Badgley and the brother of James and Eugene. (Courtesy of Frances Badgley.)

This is one of the original George Schultz residences in Murray Hill. It was located at the corner of Mountain Avenue and South Street, and was known at one time as the Van Horn residence. (Courtesy of Allstate.)

This is another George Schultz home, which was located on the corner of South Street and Oakwood Drive. It was eventually made into apartments and burned in January 1973. (Courtesy of Anita Szemes.)

The S.R. Valentine home is pictured in the top photo in 1889. It was later owned by the Attridg and Macaluso families. The lower photo is the same view and was then the Parcells-Attridg house-store combination. Notice the many changes made over the years. (Courtesy of George Lewis.)

The "Bell House," located on Springfield Avenue, west of the center of town, has an exciting history. Jim Fiske and J. Gould fled here from the Black Friday mob in the gold panic of 1869. The house was then owned by Fiske's partner, William Belden. The house takes its name from the shape of the second-story facade. (Courtesy of Anne Osborne.)

A postal card shows Mr. Jarvis Johnson's home on Springfield Avenue, where Ridgeview Avenue is now located. The Genungs later owned it, and it was torn down in 1935.

The old Noe home at 1539 Springfield Avenue is shown as it looked in 1949. (Courtesy of George Lewis.)

The Noe home was remodeled in the early 1960s by the present owners, who saw its potential! (Courtesy of Richard Kennedy.)

In November 1966, the Dickinson house was given to the historical society. It had become rundown over the years and needed much loving care. (Courtesy of Jane Parcells.)

The little "salt box" home was moved across the street to its present location with the help of many volunteers. (Courtesy of Jane Parcells.)

The museum was refurbished by its members with the help of the Borough. It is presently open to the public on a regular basis. (Courtesy of A.C. Christopher.)

Before New Providence became a borough, the Deserted Village was in our township. Although deserted for many years, it was home to a fair number of people who worked in the felt mill.

One of the fascinating aspects of the Deserted Village is its cemetery. This old gravestone is an excellent example of Revolutionary-era grave art. (Courtesy of James Hawley.)

Four
VALUE SYSTEMS

The Kendall School, *c.* 1810, was formerly the workshop of John Crane. It was moved to the intersection of Springfield and Union Avenues from his farm in Berkeley Heights. (Original photo by Sally Tiger; courtesy of Fred Best.)

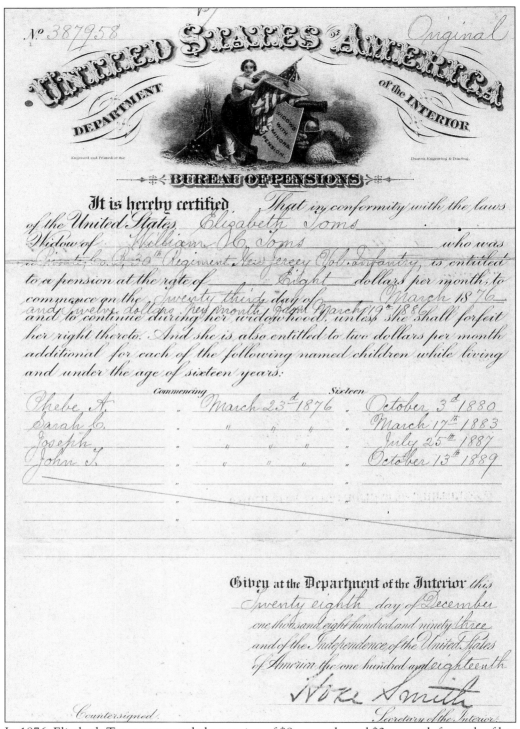

Nº 387958

UNITED STATES OF AMERICA

Original

DEPARTMENT of the INTERIOR

WIDOWS WITH MINORS PENSION

Engraved and Printed at the

Bureau Engraving & Printing.

BUREAU OF PENSIONS

It is hereby certified That in conformity with the laws of the United States _Elizabeth Toms_ . Widow of _William C. Toms_ who was _Private, Co. D, 30th Regiment New Jersey Vol. Infantry,_ is entitled to a pension at the rate of _Eight_ dollars per month, to commence on the _Twenty third day of_ _March 1876_ and _twelve dollars per month from March 19th 1886_ and to continue during her widowhood, unless she shall forfeit her right thereto. And she is also entitled to two dollars per month additional for each of the following named children while living and under the age of sixteen years:

	Commencing	Sixteen
Phebe A.	" March 23d 1876	" October 3d 1880
Sarah C.	" " "	" March 17th 1883
Joseph T.	" " "	" July 25th 1887
John T.	" " "	" October 13th 1889

Given at the Department of the Interior _this_
Twenty eighth day of _December_
one thousand eight hundred and ninety _three_
and of the Independence of the United States
of America the one hundred and _eighteenth_

Hoke Smith

Countersigned. _Secretary of the Interior._

In 1876, Elizabeth Toms was awarded a pension of $8 a month, and $2 a month for each of her four children. (Courtesy of Ora Oakwood.)

In this era, the New Providence Borough school bus was horse-drawn. (Sophie Miller, photographer; courtesy of Lucy DeCorso.)

In 1889, Mrs. Maxwell's private school was located on Springfield Avenue, in what is now the Village Shopping Center. (Courtesy of C. Lovell.)

Kindergarten came to New Providence in 1909, with Miss Inez Jessup as the first teacher. (Courtesy of George Lewis.)

The "entire" faculty of the New Providence Public Schools is shown in 1913. Pictured from left to right are Frances Burdick (principal), Marion Johnson, Helen Armstrong, E. Francis, Jane Adams, Inez Jessup, Edna Lamb, and Harriet Wilcox. (Courtesy of George Lewis.)

The old Academy bell was cast in 1873 and rang for classes until 1916. Forty-four contributors gave from $3 to $400 to have it refurbished, made to ring electronically, and replaced in the bell tower. It was used for VE Day in 1945 and at the end of World War II. (Bell: courtesy of Frank Orleans; Academy: courtesy of Jane Parcells.)

Lincoln School was opened in 1917 and used as a school until the 1980s. Field-day games were held on the front lawn in the 1930s. (Courtesy of Allen W. Roberts.)

New Providence High School was opened in 1959. Up until this time, New Providence students attended Summit High School. It became a combination middle school/high school in the early 1990s. (Courtesy of C. Coddington.)

In 1910, the Diamond Hill School housed 25 pupils of all grades. Dr. Luce was the teacher and principal. (Courtesy of Allen W. Roberts.)

Among the 1931 board of education members, shown here from left to right are: G. Balcom, Mrs. Frank Mason, Larry Winchell, Mrs. L.B. Coddington Sr., and L.B. Coddington. (Courtesy of Mrs. Frank Mason.)

Here is a postal card of the Lincoln School before any additions were needed. (Courtesy of Allen W. Roberts.)

The graduating class of 1915 poses on the steps of Lincoln School. (Courtesy of Lillian Stahl.)

Although the New Providence Memorial Library has several additions, this is the original portion. (Courtesy of Kathryn Clark.)

The Academy, built in 1869, served as a school until Lincoln School was built in 1917. The two wings are additions. It was sold for $1 to the Borough, and became our Borough Hall. (Courtesy of R.S. Kennedy.)

The cornerstone ceremony for the Hillview School took place in November 1953. Pictured here, from left to right, are Mayor Robert Badgley, Larned Meacham (cub scout), William Braunworth (president of the board of education), and Allen W. Roberts (superintendent of schools). (Courtesy of Allen W. Roberts.)

This is the New Providence Junior High School class of 1955 in their mortar boards and gowns. (Courtesy of Jane Parcells.)

A class from Lincoln School in the early 1900s shows the clothing and hair styles of the times. Jennie Mocerino Sabia is in the center row, fourth from the left. (Courtesy of Rosemarie Cucco.)

The Reverend and Mrs. Hooper are pictured here in their Sunday best. He was the pastor of the Presbyterian church from 1882 to 1905. (Courtesy of L.B. Coddington.)

The New Providence Presbyterian Church was begun in 1737. It is located at the main corner of town, with its old cemetery on the side lawn. The fire gong was the only way to alert firefighters that help was needed. The picture was taken by William Totten sometime after 1903, when the fire company was organized. (Courtesy of George Lewis.)

This summer Bible study group was studying in the summer of 1940 at the Presbyterian church. The second child in line (from the right) is Marie A. Bryan; the third is Betty Jane Wesley; the fifth is Frances May; and the twelfth is Bill Gemill. The Reverend Yerkes was pastor at the time. (Courtesy of Marie Steen.)

Pictured here are Mrs. Jane Voorhees Day, the second wife of Reverend Day, and Reverend Peter Davison Day, who was pastor of the Methodist church until he died in 1888. (Courtesy of George Lewis.)

This is a 1911 photo of the United Methodist Church, which was begun in 1786, with the initial meetings taking place in members' homes.

The Methodist Church Parsonage was photographed in 1962. The left side of the house was built in 1859, with hand-cut beams, wide floor planks, and large, Victorian-style rooms. When the house was built, a will was drawn stating that the house was never to be used by anyone except a Methodist minister. In the 1960s, the house was found unsafe, and the will was taken to court and broken so the house could be sold and a new parsonage could be built.

Charming St. Luke's Reformed Episcopal Church sits on the corner of South Street and Central Avenue. It was brought to the site on a railroad flatcar in 1891. It was a prefab built in the Ohio Valley, obviously before the era of "prefab." It has been enlarged to include a pre-school. (Courtesy of John Hickson.)

St. Andrews Episcopal Church is located on South Street on a large, tree-filled piece of property. (Courtesy of Historical Society.)

The original Our Lady of Peace Roman Catholic Church was built in 1919 on what is now the site of the Adams Shopping Center. Before the church was built, Mass was held in council chambers in the Borough Hall. (Courtesy of George Lewis.)

The groom is Anthony Ciocci and the bride is Ann Connors. Eleanor Schmidts is the maid of honor and Joe Church is the best man, at this wedding in the "old" Our Lady of Peace Church. (Courtesy of Marie Allocco.)

One of the fund-raisers for the new Catholic church was a strawberry festival. (Courtesy of A. Allocco family.)

The "new" Our Lady of Peace Church was built on a Vatican-approved plan with the congregation seated in a semi-circle. (Courtesy of Kathryn Clark.)

The Presbyterian church was the scene of the first movie shown in New Providence. If you are "of a certain age" and look closely, you may recognize some of the participants. The movies were shown around 1920 by A.G. Balcom. (Courtesy of A.G. Nason.)

The modern Faith Lutheran Church stands at the top of South Street. Built in 1957, it is the second-youngest church in town. (Courtesy of Kathryn Clark.)

Rose Ruggiero (age 16) and Theodore Beatrice (age 29) were married on March 7, 1912. Below is a copy of their marriage certificate. Rose rented her dress for $5 for the occasion. (Courtesy of Beatrice family.)

Full name of husband	*Diodoro Beatrice*					
Maiden name of wife	*Rosina Ruggiero*					
Place of marriage	*Our Lady of Mt. Carmel Church, Orange, New Jersey*					
Date of marriage	*March Seventeenth*				191 *2*	

GROOM'S	Residence	*11 Box West Summit New Jersey*			**BRIDE'S**	Residence	*204 Essex Ave. Orange New Jersey*	
	Age	*29* Yrs.	Single, Widowed or Divorced	Number of marriage		Age	*16* Yrs.	Single, Widowed or Divorced	Number of marriage
	Color	*White*		*First*		Color	*White*		*First*
	Occupation	*Laborer*				Name, if a widow		
	Birthplace	*San Marrodoi Santi (Italy)*				Birthplace	*Alborono (Italy)*	
	Father's name	*Antonio*				Father's name	*Antonio*	
	Mother's Maiden name	*Petronilla Trimondo*				Mother's maiden name	*Tranquilla De Cesare*	

Witnesses:
Diodoro Cocco
Addolorata De Palma

Signature of person or officer of society officiating and P. O. address

Rev. Leonard Borguitti

Residence of Witnesses *1170 Boulevard Jersey*
West Summit N. J.

90 Centre St. Or...

Jenny Mocerino and Vito Sabia Sr. sit with attendants for a formal wedding picture in 1926. Take note of the style of the bridal veil and the bridesmaid's hat, which were considered the "latest" at the time. (Courtesy of Sabia family.)

Vito Sabia Jr. and Elvira Mazzoni are pictured in 1940 at one of the many weddings they attended as ring bearer and flower girl. (Courtesy of Sabia family.)

Five
OLD-TIME NEIGHBORS

Mrs. Howarth organized a Maypole party with members of the Junior Endeavor at the Presbyterian church. From left to right are as follows: (first row) May Woodruff, Dayton Parcells, Linden Adams, Mabel Howarth, Howard Moll, Gussie Woodruff, Edith Adams, Rose Wireching, and Raymond Parks; (second row) George Miller, Hazel Attridg, Wallace Parcells, Lydia Blatt, and Elizabeth Attridg; (third row) Mary Jane Howarth and Edith Ripple.

In 1891, L.B. Coddington Sr. took this picture of "Uncle Eugene's Group." Pictured, from left to right, are as follows: (seated) Oscar (age 18), Jarvis (age 20), Mame (age 22), Will (age 12), and Luther (age 14); (standing) Anne Johnson Badgley (the mother), Hattie (age eight), Eugene Badgley (the father, age 41), Pauling (age four), and Sadie (age ten). (Courtesy of L.B. Coddington.)

William Hanley Badgley, son of David Badgley and great-grandfather of Gus Furneld, is pictured here with his wife, Jenette Sampson Badgley, and their daughter, Caroline Odelia Badgley. They lived at 1562 Springfield Avenue. Caroline was born in 1865. (Courtesy of George Lewis.)

George Springstine and his dog are pictured at the Millrace Bridge over South Street, where the Exxon station is now located. The photo was taken in 1891. George was killed by a train when he was a teenager. (Courtesy of George Lewis.)

Mr. and Mrs. David Totten Sr. are pictured with their son and his family. (Courtesy of Totten.)

Annie Johnson Badgely, dressed in her bicycling outfit, prepares for an afternoon jaunt. (Courtesy of Thomas Badgley.)

Men's attire (note the knickers) made bicycling more simple. Pictured here is Lyman Coddington. (Courtesy of George Lewis.)

Dayton Badgley, a town father, was the great-grandfather of Elsie Jacobus. (Courtesy of George Lewis.)

Tom Scott, standing with the printing press of the 1890s, became editor of the *Passaic Valley News*. (Courtesy of John Peck.)

Maude Dickinson (Mrs. Halsey Genung) poses for a professional photographer. (Courtesy of John Peck.)

Jane Noe Totten Howarth, 22 years old, and her one-year-old daughter, Grace Edna Howarth, are seen here, in 1904, in the side yard of the Totten home on Elkwood Avenue. (Courtesy of Elsie Klemser.)

Seated in the garden with their grandson, Leon Parcells, are the Badgley grandparents. The baby's mother is Margaret Badgley Parcells. (Courtesy of Frances Badgley.)

Mr. and Mrs. Potter and their son, Amos, are posed in a formal setting. Note the lamp and table covering which suggests the Victorian era. (Courtesy of Herbert High.)

Members of the Nason family pose on their front steps in 1902. Family members include Dr. and Mrs. Wilcox and Mr. and Mrs. Walter Kyritzes. (Courtesy of Allen W. Roberts.)

In 1951, Rosemarie Sabia married Bill Cucco at Our Lady of Peace Church. (Courtesy of Rosemarie Sabia Cucco.)

The Cucco children are pictured in 1934. From left to right are James, Louis, Marie, Bill, and Elinor (in the front-center). (Courtesy of Rosemarie Cucco.)

Many volunteered during the Spanish-American War. Included here are John Peck, Alfred Kent (who later became Summit's postmaster), and Dr. Rively (seated at the far right). (Courtesy of John Peck.)

A float bearing a red cross made of Coddington roses was made for a Memorial Day parade during WW II. (Courtesy of George Lewis.)

A memorial stone is shown veiled and unveiled on the Presbyterian church property during the July 4th celebration in 1919. The stone, with veterans' names inscribed, still sits in a place of honor in the center of town. (Courtesy of Sophie Miller.)

Local women joined the "Woman's Land Army of America" and worked at truck farms in the surrounding towns. (Courtesy of George Lewis.)

Mary Krayer, Elsie Parcells, Helen Armstrong, Jeannette Burn, and Edie Adams were hired to husk fields of corn. The men were at war, and there was a flu epidemic during this time in 1918, so few were available for work. (Courtesy of George Lewis.)

Harry High and Patsy Annelli, in the fourth window, are off to WW I. (Courtesy of Bertha High.)

Carl Totten is seen here in his WW I uniform. (Courtesy of Sophie Miller.)

The "Original Bunch" of Boy Scouts are shown in 1927. Among those pictured are, from left to right: (front row) David Fitzinger, Freddie Parse, Karl Mason, Donald Totten, Robert Kelly, Joe Meci, Roger Campbell, Chester Lambert, and James Hogg; (back row) Perry Adams, Everett Schenk, Harold Webster, Stephen Nichols, Walton Osborne, and Walter Behre. (Courtesy of Bob Schwarzwalder.)

Philomena Zotti and Grace Parliapiano march at the head of the band. (Courtesy of Marie Allocco.)

Local Boy Scouts enjoyed camping at this Great Swamp camp during the 1940s. (Courtesy of Bob Schwarzwalder.)

Seen in Stokes Forest, in 1941, are, from left to right: Bob Schlichting, Bill Spurgeon, Bob Hamilton, and Roy Putnam. (Courtesy of Bob Schwarzwalder.)

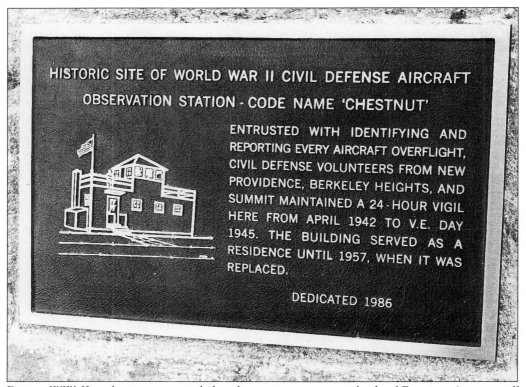

HISTORIC SITE OF WORLD WAR II CIVIL DEFENSE AIRCRAFT OBSERVATION STATION - CODE NAME 'CHESTNUT'

ENTRUSTED WITH IDENTIFYING AND REPORTING EVERY AIRCRAFT OVERFLIGHT, CIVIL DEFENSE VOLUNTEERS FROM NEW PROVIDENCE, BERKELEY HEIGHTS, AND SUMMIT MAINTAINED A 24-HOUR VIGIL HERE FROM APRIL 1942 TO V.E. DAY 1945. THE BUILDING SERVED AS A RESIDENCE UNTIL 1957, WHEN IT WAS REPLACED.

DEDICATED 1986

During WW II, volunteers manned the observation station in back of Fairview Avenue, off Central Avenue. (Courtesy of Bertha Roberts Nason.)

Local scrap collections played a big part in the war effort. Many tons were collected by the residents of the Borough. (Courtesy of Mary M. Mason.)

Pictured from left to right are: Reverend Dabinet, Mayor Oakwood, William Webster, and Reverend Yerkes, at the dedication of the Borough Honor Roll for WW II. (Courtesy of Mrs. Ora Oakwood.)

As part of the Memorial Day celebration in 1942, the Boy Scouts organized an elaborate tableau. Sam Jones (who later became mayor) was the scout leader. (Courtesy of Bill Spurgeon.)

Anthony (Tony) J. Ciocci is pictured in his Veterans-of-Foreign-Wars cap. (Courtesy of Marie Allocco.)

A Victory Garden, maintained by school children prior to 1948, was on the land where Gales Drive Apartments now stand. (Courtesy of Allen W. Roberts.)

In 1959, the Mason's backyard was the site of the Senior Citizens Picnic. Pictured from left to right are: (seated) Florence Spicer, Minnie Bradley, Margaret Davis, Mary Mason, Elsie Herse, and Jock Geigerich; (standing) Jean Nadele, Arlie Jones, Katherine Stein, Sue Hoffmann, Arthur Minner, Elsie Lull, Frank Kossuth (from the church recreation commission), Marie Stadler, Mrs. Munson (a visitor from England), Catherine Geigerich, Sadie Kitchell, Ada Kecker, Nancy Bartfai, Annette Tannery, Andrew Bartfai (director of recreation), and Mrs. Noll. (Courtesy of Mary Mason.)

This was Mr. and Mrs. Howard's golden anniversary. (Courtesy of John Peck.)

Bob, Gene, and Jr. Egbert were photographed in 1933. They lived at the corner of Elkwood and Academy Streets. (Courtesy of George Lewis.)

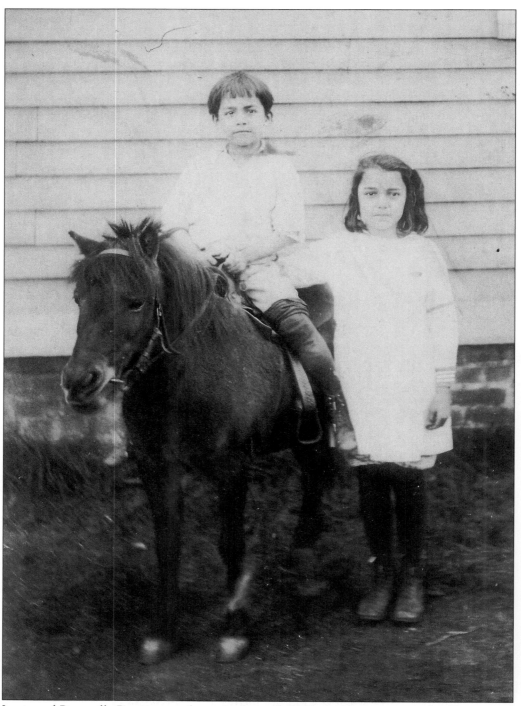

Lucio and Petronilla Beatrice are shown in the early 1920s, enjoying a pony ride. (Courtesy of Tran Beatrice.)

Six
FUN TIMES

Lester Genung is ready for the Fourth-of-July parade, around 1910. (Courtesy of John Hickson.)

Harold and Horace Guerin and Margaret Adams are dressed in colonial costumes for the Fourth-of-July parade. (Courtesy of Anne Osborne.)

Mary Baldwin and Dr. Dayton Baldwin proceed down Springfield Avenue. Note the umbrellas screening the onlookers. (Courtesy of John Hickson.)

Cars, new to New Providence, stir up dirt on the unpaved Springfield Avenue in the Fourth-of-July parade in 1911. (Courtesy of John Hickson.)

Ardell Osborne Fleming won second prize for her decorative carriage in the July 4, 1911 parade.

Decorated carriages are headed toward the judges stand. Whole families participated in this event. (Courtesy of John Hickson.)

Arthur Peck and Margaret Adams look unenthusiastic about their part of the day. (Courtesy of John Hickson.)

Participants in the 1922 Fourth-of-July celebration pass in front of 1161 and 1167 Springfield Avenue. (Courtesy of Allen W. Roberts.)

Volunteer firemen march in the Memorial Day parade in the 1940s. From left to right, marchers are as follows: (front row) Robert Webster Sr., Henry Pictroski, Elmer Ayres, and Dayton Parcells; (second row) Walter Behre, Theodore Bahr, Harry Williamson, and Walton Osborne. The first house is a four-family home—Attridg, Malluso, and Weid once lived there. Ernie Fischer drives the truck. (Courtesy of Jane Parcells.)

A crowd is gathered for ceremonies at the Memorial Day parade in 1940. Arthur Paradise and child are pictured in the lower right-hand corner. (Courtesy of Allen W. Roberts.)

Jean Radtke Peotter is the Girl Scout to the left. George Egerton and Tom Traiola are carrying the colors in the 1942 Memorial Day parade. (Courtesy of Bob Schwarzwalder.)

The parade turns the corner at the Presbyterian church. (Courtesy of Sophie Miller.)

Art Miller and Kenneth Totten try to slide on a very tiny hill in back of Lincoln School. (Courtesy of Sophie Miller.)

January 1908

Sleigh-riding was popular on Livingston Avenue in 1908. There is not a house in sight! (Courtesy of Anne Osborne.)

Aggie Nevins, Grace Valentine Balcom, and Mary Badgley rest in front of the Dickenson's house after a tennis match. (Courtesy of Frances Badgley.)

A New Providence 1901 baseball team poses for a team picture. (Courtesy of Mrs. Peck.)

Pictured here is the Pine Grove Athletic Club basketball team which played in Pine Grove Hall (Osborne's Hall). The clubhouse was on Passaic Street on the bank of the Passaic River. (Courtesy of John Hickson.)

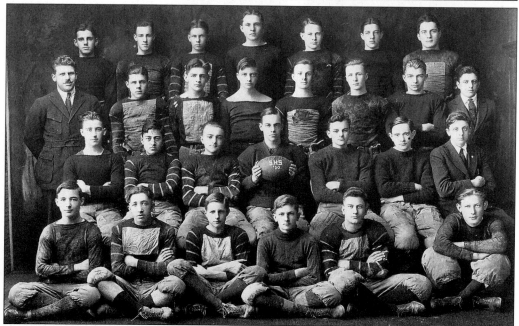

The 1920 Summit football team included many members from New Providence. Our students attended Summit High School until 1959, when New Providence opened its own high school. (Courtesy of Frances Badgley.)

This is the New Providence Athletic Club baseball team as it appeared in 1910. From left to right are as follows: (front row) Bobbie Brown, Harold Ahern, George Williamson, Jimmy Cribbins, and Bill Totten; (back row) Bob Frazer, Herbert Wilcox, Leon Parcells (assistant manager), Mr. Balcom (manager), Art Futten, and Bill Knight. (Courtesy of Parcells family.)

Ice skating was very popular at some of the "ponds" in town. (Courtesy of R.S. Kennedy.)

In 1910, the baseball team traveled with many spectators to Basking Ridge (upper photo). The photo below pictures the team on its way home after the game. (Courtesy of Sophie Miller.)

This baseball field with grandstand was on Passaic Street, behind the Presbyterian Parish House, in the early 1920s. The upper photo shows the dedication of the flagpole at the ball park. (Courtesy of John Hickson and George Lewis.)

Sports for women were limited. There was, however, a volleyball team, including, from left to right: Anne Badgley, Mary Dickerson Maxwell, Helen Armstrong, Pauline Badgley, Mabel Brower Peck, Harriet Badgley, and Inez Jessup. (Courtesy of Robert Badgley.)

There was a race track in New Providence near Jane Road and Springfield Avenue which was built by David L. Osborne. Luther Badgley is shown on the track. (Courtesy of Anne Osborne.)

In December 1951, the last organized deer-hunting party took place in New Providence. Hunting was prohibited the next year due to the development of residential areas. The photographer was Jules Bystrak, who was a member of the hunting party. (Courtesy of C. Ernie Fischer.)

A stylish group of beachgoers from New Providence enjoy a day at the New Jersey shore. (Courtesy of John Hickson.)

The Pavilion on the Passaic River was once owned by David L. Osborne. It was also where, in 1912, Frederick H. Kammerer met his future wife.

This photo was taken in 1892 by Elizabeth Barrell. It shows two Barrell girls with "the hired man" boating on the Passaic. (Courtesy of George Lewis.)

An old-fashioned, picturesque group of young women gathered for a sunny afternoon. From left to right are as follows: (first row) Alice and Gertrude Hickey (Helen High's cousins); (second row) Ida Van Nostrand; (third row) Mabel Brower, Lillian Totten, and Helen High. (Courtesy of George Lewis.)

In 1911 or 1912, the Parcells and Attridg families gathered for a picnic after church. From left to right are as follows: Mr. and Mrs. A.G. Balcom, Mr. and Mrs. John Peck, George Attridg (behind J. Peck), Mr. and Mrs. Samuel Parcells, Dayton Parcells, and Mr. and Mrs. Attridg with their three daughters. (Courtesy of John Peck.)

In July 1931, these three New Providence ladies traveled to the shore for an outing in the sun and sand. From left to right are: Helen Armstrong, Mrs. Armstrong (Helen's mother), and Mrs. Thomas Crane. (Courtesy of A.W. Roberts.)

In the late 1800s, a group of friends celebrated Amy Lovell's birthday with silly hats and what appears to be fake cigars. Pictured here, from left to right, are as follows: (front row) unidentified and Florence Badgley Cornish; (middle row) Elizabeth Wilcox, Sarah Badgley Moreland, Adeline Badgley Wood, Pauline Badgley, and unidentified; (back row) unidentified, Clara Lovell Snyder, Harriette Badgley, and Amy Lovell.